GERMANY

In the Heartland of Europe

SWEDEN

DENMARK

NORTH
SEA

BALTIC SEA

SCHLESWIG-
HOLSTEIN

MECKLENBURG-
WEST POMERANIA

Hamburg

Elbe

Oder

POLAND

Bremen

Weser

LOWER SAXONY

Berlin

NETHERLANDS

BRANDENBURG

Hameln

NORTH
RHINE-WESTPHALIA

SAXONY-ANHALT

Essen

Ruhr R.

Harz
Range

Leipzig

Düsseldorf

Kassel

Weser

SAXONY

Cologne

Meissen

Bonn

Weimar

Dresden

Aachen

HESSE

THURINGIA

BELGIUM

Rhine

Lahn

RHINELAND-
PALATINATE

Frankfurt

Hanau

CZECH
REPUBLIC

LUX.

Moselle

Würzburg

Main

Bayreuth

Bohemian Forest

SAARLAND

Fürth im
Wald

Speyer

Nuremberg

Saar R.

BAVARIA

Ettlingen

Stuttgart

Danube

N

Rhine

Black Forest

BADEN-
WÜRTTEMBERG

Dachau

FRANCE

Munich

Starnbergersee

AUSTRIA

Freiburg

Oberammergau

Capital city

Garmisch-
Partenkirchen

Bavarian Alps

Major town

Lake
Constance

Mountain peak

Zugspitze
(9,731 ft)

Feet   Meters

SWITZERLAND

16,000   4,880

10,000   3,050

LIECHTENSTEIN

6,000   1,830

GERMANY

3,000   910

1,500   460

Scale 1:4,500,000

600   180

0   0

0   50   100 Miles

ITALY

0   50   100   150 Kilometers

© Oxford Cartographers

GERMANY

In the Heartland of Europe

Eleanor H. Ayer

BENCHMARK BOOKS

MARSHALL CAVENDISH

NEW YORK

With thanks to Christina Breede of
Deutsches Haus, Columbia University, New York City,
for her expert reading of the manuscript,
and to the staff and students at Deutsche Schule in
White Plains, New York, for their assistance in research.

Benchmark Books
Marshall Cavendish Corporation
99 White Plains Road
Tarrytown, New York 10591-9001

© Marshall Cavendish Corporation 1996

Library of Congress Cataloging-in-Publication Data
Ayer, Eleanor H., date.
  Germany / by Eleanor H. Ayer.
      p.   cm. — (Exploring cultures of the world)
  Includes bibliographical references.
  ISBN 0-7614-0189-X (lib. binding)
  1. Germany—Juvenile literature. [1. Germany.]   I. Title.   II. Series.
DD17.A94   1996
943—dc20   95-15341

SUMMARY: Discusses the history, geography, daily life, culture, and customs of Germany.

Printed and bound in Italy

Book design by Carol Matsuyama
Photo research by Debbie Needleman

Photo Credits
Front cover and page 40: courtesy of IFA/Peter Arnold; back cover and pages 6, 8, 10, 18, 35, 52: courtesy of Bob Krist; title page: courtesy of Ben Simmons/The Stock Market; page 9: The Bettmann Archive; pages 12, 22, 27, 34, 43: B. W. Hoffmann /Envision; page 13: Scala/Art Resource, NY; page 14: Giraudon /Art Resource, NY; page 15: Art Resource, NY; pages 20, 25: Michael J. Howell/Envision; page 28: Horst Schafer/Peter Arnold; page 30: AP/Wide World Photos; pages 32, 39, 57: Dave Bartruff; page 33: Sylvain Granadam/Tony Stone Images; page 37: Kevin Galvin/The Stock Market; page 45: Joachim Messerschmidt /Bruce Coleman; page 46: UPI/Bettmann; page 48: Christopher Wood Gallery, London/Bridgeman Art Library, London; pages 50, 53: Erich Lessing/Art Resource, NY; page 54: SEF/Art Resource, NY; page 55: Joe Bator/The Stock Market; page 56: Bonhams, London/Bridgeman Art Library, London

Contents

Linderhof, one of the many castles built by Ludwig II of Bavaria

1

GEOGRAPHY AND HISTORY

Germany: Past and Present

He was called "Mad" Ludwig, not because he was angry but because he was crazy—or so people said. For twenty-two years beginning in 1864, Ludwig II was king of Bavaria, a mountainous state in southern Germany. While he was king he spent huge amounts of royal money building fairy-tale castles in the Bavarian Alps.

Ludwig hated the politics and paperwork of running a kingdom. Instead he preferred to dream about fancy palaces, fountains, costumes, and carriages—and to attend the operas of German composer Richard Wagner. Ludwig's favorite opera was Lohengrin, the story of a knight who came to earth in a boat drawn by a magical swan.

Many of Ludwig's castles and courtyards were designed with Wagner's operas in mind. The smallest of them, Linderhof, was the only one finished during the king's lifetime. Its jewel-like rooms are decorated in gold and marble, and from their ceilings hang countless crystal chandeliers. In the dining room is a table that can be lowered into the kitchens on the floor below, then raised again. Statues made of bronze and beautiful porcelain stand near fireplaces fitted with

A swan boat floats on the pond in front of the Blue Grotto at Linderhof Castle.

semiprecious gemstones. Not far from the castle Ludwig built a massive cave called the Blue Grotto. On certain days he would dress in the shining armor of the swan-knight, Lohengrin, and stand with a sword at his side while a swan boat carried him around the pond in front of the Blue Grotto.

Many of the king's fairy-tale creations were built near Schwangau (SHVAHN-gow), the "swan region" of far southwestern Bavaria. Here, hidden in the forest, is the royal castle of Hohenschwangau, where Ludwig spent much of his childhood. Across the valley from Hohenschwangau, on a high mountain peak, is the spot the king chose for his masterpiece, Neuschwanstein (noy-SHVAHN-shtain) castle. Neuschwanstein took seventeen years to construct and later became the model for the castle in Walt Disney's Sleeping Beauty as well as for the Magic Kingdom castle.

Ghostly cavelike hallways connect Neuschwanstein's many turrets and towers with its finely furnished rooms. The castle's highlight is the two-story throne room, its rich blue ceiling filled with a thousand twinkling stars. Saints and angels peer down from solid gold walls. A huge piece of artwork shows Christ floating in the skies among a group of kings, while the twelve disciples offer them advice. The floor is fitted with stone to form a beautiful pattern of plants and animals.

A flight of marble stairs leads to the spot where a throne is supposed to stand. But there is no throne at Neuschwanstein. Ludwig died before it could be installed. In June 1886, under pressure from the Bavarian government, a team of doctors declared the king insane. Despite his protests, Ludwig was taken to Berg castle on Lake Starnberg. There, on the evening of June 13, he and Dr. Bernhard von Gudden, who was in charge of Ludwig, went for a walk. No one

King Ludwig II of Bavaria. Some people called him "Mad" Ludwig because they thought he was crazy.

9

Neuschwanstein Castle, King Ludwig's masterpiece

knows what happened, but the next morning, their bodies were found floating near the shore of the lake.

Today a cross stands at the spot in the lake where the "dream king" drowned. Though he was called crazy in his time and was hated for spending huge amounts of money on his dreams, Ludwig's castles are now one of the greatest tourist attractions in Germany. Neuschwanstein and Hohenschwangau alone receive more than a million visitors a year.

The German Landscape

Bavaria, called Bayern (BAI-ehrn) in German, where the great castles of King Ludwig II still stand, is the largest of the sixteen states, or *Länder*, that make up Germany. The high, snow-covered peaks of the Alps; the lush, green mountain meadows; and the crystal-clear alpine lakes make Bavaria one of the prettiest places in Germany.

Germany is in the center of Europe. Its southern border meets the Alps of Austria and Switzerland. Its northern tip forms a peninsula with Denmark, surrounded by the North and Baltic Seas. To the east lie Poland and the Czech Republic, and on the west are France and the Low Countries of Belgium, Luxembourg, and the Netherlands. Germany makes a "footprint" on the globe about twice as big as the state of Washington.

As it stretches northward more than 500 miles (805 kilometers), the German countryside changes from the high mountains and foothills of the south to the plains and river basins in the center, known as the Central Uplands. After crossing the Harz Mountain range, midway through the country, the land begins to slope away in what is called the North German Lowland, heading toward the seas.

Each of these regions has a different kind of weather and climate. The heaviest rainfall and the coldest temperatures are in the south. The Uplands region in the center of the country is usually milder. But in the Black Forest of the far southwest and in the Harz Mountains of central Germany, winters are cold and snowy. Along the Rhine and Moselle Rivers in the west, the climate is mild enough for lush vineyards to produce grapes that make world-famous German wine. In the Lowland region of the north, the land is flat or slightly hilly,

11

Many vineyards dot the banks of the Rhine River. World-famous German wines are made from the grapes grown here.

and the weather often depends on the mood of the ocean. Winter temperatures there hover around freezing, and summer temperatures average 65°F (18°C).

The climate in the mountainous regions of Germany makes the perfect home for one of Europe's most remarkable animals—the wild boar, a powerful beast with a black, bristly body, sharp tusks, and a long snout. It was once the object of chases by large hunting parties. The head of this fierce mammal—ancestor of today's pigs—was said to be a real delicacy, particularly when roasted in wine and served on a huge platter at ceremonies in the castles and hunting lodges of Bavaria. Now civilization and overhunting have endangered this amazing animal.

Germany, Long Ago

About two thousand years ago many different tribes of people roamed the land that is now Deutschland (DOYCH-lahnt), or Germany. Today the boundaries of some of the *Länder* run approximately where the different tribes roamed. The most powerful group was the Franks. Their king, Charlemagne, brought the tribes together, and in A.D. 800 he became the first emperor of the Holy Roman Empire. This huge empire included not only Germany but other countries of modern-day Europe. The Holy Roman Empire lasted for ten centuries, and during much of that time it was ruled by German emperors.

Over the centuries the empire grew weaker. Certain smaller regions decided to break away and govern themselves. In many areas people waged wars over religion. One of the greatest religious upheavals began in 1517, when Martin

This seventeenth-century painting shows a fearsome wild boar and its babies being chased by a hunter and his dogs.

13

Charlemagne, first emperor of the Holy Roman Empire, in a painting by German artist Albrecht Dürer

Luther, a German monk, attacked the ideas of the Roman Catholic Church. Because Luther was protesting the teachings of the Church, he and his followers were called Protestants. This period of protest, called the Reformation, lasted for much of the sixteenth century. It led to the bloody battles known as the Thirty Years' War. When that war ended in 1648, Germany was nearly destroyed, and the Holy Roman Empire was split into 350 separate states.

It took Germany nearly one hundred years to recover. By the early 1700s the state of Prussia was becoming very strong. In 1740 a great king, Frederick II, came to power in Prussia. During the forty-six years of his rule, Frederick the Great helped this northern state, and its capital at Berlin, to become more powerful. The leaders who followed him captured new lands and fought back Austria, which was trying to gain control of the German states.

When the bold and brilliant

*Portrait of
Martin Luther,
founder of
Protestantism*

Otto von Bismarck became prime minister of Prussia in 1862, he promised to use "blood and iron" to unite Germany. He enlarged and strengthened the Prussian army, fought three small wars, and by 1871 had made his promise come true. Germany was united under its first emperor, Kaiser Wilhelm I, and Bismarck was its first chancellor, the head of government.

Germany in Modern Times

This was the start of a wonderful new age for Germany. The country traded much more with other nations and also developed its natural resources. Scientists and scholars made great advances in learning. Kaiser Wilhelm II, who became emperor in 1888, built the army and navy into the most powerful forces the world had ever known.

But the rest of Europe was getting nervous. Other countries feared Germany's growing power. In 1914 those fears erupted into World War I. Four years later, when the war ended, the once proud and prosperous Germany lay in tatters. The world blamed Germany for starting the war and punished it with harsh peace terms. The German people had to pay huge amounts of money to the countries that had suffered most in the war. Military leaders were ordered not to rebuild the army and navy. No one wanted the German nation to become so powerful again.

During the next fifteen years Germany sank to one of the lowest points in its history. People had no money, no jobs, and no hope for the future. Then came a leader who promised to restore national pride and make Germany a powerful nation once again. Adolf Hitler, leader of the Nazi party, became chancellor in 1933. For a time Hitler was a hero. He put Germans back to work and the country began to grow. But by 1939 *der Führer* (dehr FYIH-rehr), the leader, had plunged his people into World War II.

At the end of that war in 1945 the country once more lay in ashes. Hitler was dead by suicide, and again Germans were accused of having started a world war. But this time they were burdened with something even more horrible: the Holocaust. The world learned that millions of innocent people had died or been killed in the Nazis' concentration camps. In shame the Germans realized what a tremendous price they had paid for following Adolf Hitler.

The world did not punish Germany as harshly after this war as it had after World War I. The United States helped Germany to recover by giving the government money and supplies. The German people dug into the rubble of their ruined cities, scraped mortar off old bricks, straightened boards, and began rebuilding their country and their lives. Within a few years the country was on its way up again.

But there was still a scar on Deutschland. At the end of the war, American, British, French, and Russian troops occupied parts of Germany. Their job was to help the Germans rebuild and to be sure they followed the terms for peace. The areas occupied by England, France, and the United States became West Germany. Russia, under the Communists, controlled East Germany. The capital, Berlin, was also split into free and Communist sections. For forty-one years Germany remained divided. At last, in 1990, when Communist rule in other European countries began to fail, West Germany and East Germany again united into one Germany.

GERMAN GOVERNMENT

Germany is a federal republic and has three branches of government. The legislative branch, or parliament, is called the *Bundesregierung.* Its job is to pass laws, and it is made up of two chambers: the *Bundestag* (House of Representatives), which has approximately 660 members, and the *Bundesrat* (Federal Council), which has a maximum of 68 members.

The head of the executive branch of government is the chancellor. He is the leader of the party that is elected to power. There is also a president, but his position is less powerful than that of the chancellor. Helmut Kohl is the current chancellor, and he has been in power since 1984, longer than any other chancellor in the twentieth century.

In the judicial branch of government, the highest court is the Constitutional Court. It is similar to the Supreme Court in the United States. The job of this court is to make decisions on questions about the Basic Law, Germany's constitution.

This woman is from Bavaria, the German state known for its quiet, colorful villages.

2

Who Are
the Germans?

If your last name is Miller or Smith, the chances are good that one of your ancestors was German. Müller and Schmidt are two of the most common last names in Germany. Other common family names are Fischer, Weber, and Maier. These names—and others, like Hoffman, Schneider, Schultz, and Wagner—are common in America because, since the early 1800s, many Germans have immigrated, moved to, the United States.

In many German last names, the word *von* appears before the main name. Paul von Hindenburg (former president of Germany), Manfred von Richthofen (World War I pilot), and composer Carl Maria von Weber are a few examples. In German *von* means "of" or "from." Long ago this word was put into some last names to show where a person was from. Later *von* came to mean that a person had wealth, or importance, or was from a higher class. Today the word is being used less and less.

Where Do Deutschlanders Live?
More than eighty million people live in Deutschland today.

That's about the same as the number of people who live in California, New York, Texas, and Illinois combined. Yet in land size, Germany isn't even as big as the state of Montana. That means it is densely populated—one of the most crowded countries in Europe.

Germany's population is not spread evenly across the country. About a third lives in large cities of more than 100,000. The largest, Berlin, is expected to double in size by the year 2000, as government offices move there from Bonn. Hamburg, a port on the North Sea, is Germany's second largest city.

Another densely populated part of the country is in the

A view of the beautiful medieval city of Heidelberg

west, near the cities of Essen and Düsseldorf. This area, where the Rhine and Ruhr Rivers meet, is home to more than four million people. So close together are the towns that it's hard to tell where one stops and the next begins.

Two out of every three Germans live in rural areas or small cities. Former East Germany is more sparsely populated (less crowded) than the west. Rugged southern Bavaria is also sparsely populated. This area is known for its quiet, colorful little villages. Mountain huts and hunting lodges dot the forests.

Who Is a "Typical" German?

An imaginary line, running roughly through the city of Frankfurt, separates northern Germans from southern. In the north people are apt to have blond hair and blue eyes, and to follow the Protestant faith. These are hardworking people. They are what the rest of the world often thinks of as typical Germans. South of Frankfurt, people are somewhat more carefree. They are likely to have dark hair and brown eyes, and to be Roman Catholic. Still, it is important to remember that you can find both Protestants and Catholics, both blond-haired and dark-haired people, living throughout Germany today.

Germans are known for being on time, being well organized, and paying attention to details. In many of their folk songs, passed down over the years, they show a great love for nature and the outdoors. But because of war-loving leaders in the country's past, Germans also have been considered militaristic. This means that they wish to be powerful and rule by force.

Some Germans are called xenophobic (zehn-uh-FO-bihk), meaning that they fear and dislike foreigners. During the 1950s

21

One of the pretty country houses in Bavaria

and 1960s many *Gastarbeiter* (guest workers) came to Germany from foreign countries to work in factories. Hatred grew between some Germans and the *Gastarbeiter*, especially those from Turkey. Since the unification in 1990, there have been attacks on

GERMANS WHO CHANGED THE WORLD

Attila the Hun (406?–453). King of the Huns, a warlike tribe that lived in central Europe and savagely conquered other tribes. During World War I enemy soldiers called German soldiers "the Hun," after Attila and his men.

Johannes Gutenberg (1390–1468). German inventor who designed movable metal type and the printing press. These inventions made it possible to print many books at a time. Before this people had to copy books by hand. In about 1456 Gutenberg printed the first Bible from movable type.

Johannes Kepler (1571–1630). Mathematician and astronomer who discovered the basic rules of gravity. He proved that planets travel in orbits around the sun.

Gabriel Daniel Fahrenheit (1686–1736). First to use mercury in thermometers as a way to measure temperature more exactly. The Fahrenheit temperature scale is named for him.

Karl Marx (1818–1883) and **Friedrich Engels** (1820–1895). Called the fathers of modern communism. Together they published the *Communist Manifesto.* It shows how working-class people can gain power by revolting against the government. Marx also published *Das Kapital,* a book about the struggle between rich people and poor workers.

Paul Ehrlich (1854–1915). Scientist who studied bacteria that cause diseases. He helped find cures and ways to prevent diseases such as diphtheria; was the founder of chemotherapy, the use of chemicals to help stop the spread of cancer.

Albert Einstein (1879–1955). A genius in the science of physics. Einstein is best known for his theory of relativity and its formula, $E=mc^2$. It was this theory that made it possible for scientists to build the atomic bomb.

Adolf Hitler (1889–1945). Leader of Nazi Germany who became the world's symbol of evil. He led Germany into World War II and built concentration and death camps where millions of innocent people were sent to be killed or worked to death.

Wernher von Braun (1912–1977). Scientist who built a rocket-propelled bomb used by the Germans in World War II. After the war he came to the United States to work for the army. Developed the first U.S. satellite, *Explorer 1,* which was launched in 1958.

foreigners. Many of the attackers are young people. The German government is trying hard to stop this violence. In school, children are given books, tapes, films, and pamphlets about xenophobia.

Sprechen Sie Deutsch?

If you do speak German, answer *"Ja."* If you don't, say *"Nein."* Today more than 100 million people speak German. It is the main language of Germany, Austria, and the tiny country of Liechtenstein (LIHK-tuhn-shtain). It is also one of the official languages of Switzerland.

SAY IT IN GERMAN

Here is how you would say some common words and phrases in German:

yes	*ja* (yah)
no	*nein* (nain)
please	*bitte* (BIH-teh)
thank you	*danke* (DAHN-keh)
hello	*guten tag* (GOO-tn TAHK)
good-bye	*auf wiedersehen* (ahf VEE-dehr-zeh-hehn)
one	*ein* (ain)
Sunday	*Sonntag* (ZOHN-tahk)

Here is an old German proverb:

Wer den Pfennig nicht ehrt ist des Thalers nicht wert.
Which means: "He who doesn't appreciate the pfennig is not worthy of the thaler."

The deutsche mark has replaced the old thaler in the German money system, but the message remains the same. In English we might say, "A person who doesn't know the value of a penny doesn't deserve a dollar."

Most people in Germany speak "pure," or High German. Low German is the same language, but with different accents and phrases and some different words. The different ways of speaking are called dialects. As you travel around the country, you hear different dialects spoken, especially by older people.

You may have noticed that some German words have two little dots over certain vowels. This mark is called an umlaut, and it changes the way that letter is pronounced. For example the word for "under" is *unter* (OON-tehr), but the word for "over" is *über* (UE-behr). To make this different sound of *u*, make your lips very round and say *ee*. You may

Turkish residents of Stuttgart. In recent years these "guest workers" and their families have been the targets of German xenophobia—an intense dislike and fear of foreigners.

25

also have noticed that in German, all nouns (words that name a person, place, or thing) are capitalized. If we used this rule in English, a sentence would look like this: *The Boy threw a big Bone to his Dog.*

Religion in Germany

Four out of every ten Germans are Roman Catholic. Slightly more than that are Protestant. In the Protestant north most people are Lutheran—followers of reformer Martin Luther. In the south they are generally Roman Catholic. Ten million Germans say that they have no religion at all.

The arrival of the guest workers from Turkey in the 1950s and 1960s brought another religion into Germany. Today there are nearly two million Muslims in the country, most of them Turkish.

Before 1933, when the Nazis came to power, more than half a million Jews lived in Germany. But nearly two out of every three Jews died during the Holocaust. Many of those who survived decided never to live in Germany again. Today only forty thousand Germans are Jewish.

Craftsmen, Brewers, and Farmers

Years ago, in the Black Forest region of southwestern Germany, farmers spent cold winter evenings carving fancy figures out of wood. Of all their products the beautifully carved cuckoo clocks were the finest. Today clock making is no longer done by farmers but by German companies, which sell famous Black Forest cuckoo clocks all over the world.

Meissen, a small town in eastern Germany, is known for another special craft. In 1709 the ruler August the Strong ordered his court chemists to find the formula for making

A wood carver puts the final touches on a piece of craftwork.

gold. None of the chemists succeeded, but one of them, Johann Friedrich Böttger, found a way to produce porcelain, the material from which fine dishes are made. Within a year craftsmen at Meissen were making dishes and other pretty pieces from Böttger's "white gold." Nearly three hundred years later this fine porcelain is still produced in Meissen and sold around the world.

Another world-famous German product is beer. Forty percent of all beer made in the world comes from Germany's thirteen hundred breweries. Some are huge companies; others are set up in the cellars of farmhouses. Among them they make more than five thousand different kinds of beer. So proud are Germans of their beer that brewers must obey a law that says that every drop must be of the highest quality.

Nearly as famous as German beer is German wine. Along the banks of the Moselle, Saar, and Rhine Rivers in the west,

Hop harvesting is a time for celebration in Germany. The hops are used to make the country's world-famous beers.

there are many vineyards. The climate there is perfect for growing grapes, and the white wines bottled in this region are some of the best in the world.

Grapes are just one of Germany's many crops. About half

the land is used for farming. Farmers produce much of the food the country needs. One farmer can raise enough to feed more than seventy people. Farmers don't make much money, however, so many of them also work full time at other jobs.

Germany: An Industrial Giant

More than 7.5 million Germans work at industrial jobs—building equipment, machinery, or other products in factories. The building of cars is Germany's biggest industry. There are also huge companies that produce chemicals and medicines. Some of the largest electronics businesses in the world, like the giant Bosch company, are German owned. The country is also known for its high-quality cameras made by Leica. Specialized tools and instruments that doctors or engineers use come from the Zeiss company.

In the north, around Hamburg, shipbuilding is an important industry. To the west, the densely populated Rhine-Ruhr region is the center of manufacturing. Here giant factories once turned the sky black with their smoke. In recent years Germans have become very worried about pollution and have taken steps to clean up their air and water.

The biggest and most successful companies are in western Germany. The east, where the Communists once controlled all business, lags far behind. Factory buildings there are old and crumbling. Machinery is outdated and breaks down often. The few factories that are still open spit out smoke and chemicals that pollute the air and water. The west is now working to improve conditions in the east, but the problems are huge and need much money to correct.

This eighteen-year-old girl wears a traditional German dress on her way to vote for the first time.

3

FAMILY LIFE, FESTIVALS, AND FOOD

Every Day and Special Days

Germerman kids are not very different from American kids. They wear jeans and T-shirts, play soccer and hide-and-seek, ride bicycles, and like dolls and computer games. McDonald's and the other fast-food restaurant chains are nearly as popular in Germany as they are in the United States, even though Germans don't eat out as often.

A Typical Family's Schedule

German children's daily routines are also similar to those of American kids. School generally begins at 8:00. At about 10:30, students take a snack or sandwich break. Elementary school is out for the day at noon. Secondary school runs about an hour longer.

In German homes the big meal is at midday, right after school. Fathers who work close by go home for *Mittagessen* (the noon meal). Women usually fix the meals because fewer of them work outside the home than women in America do. During the afternoon German children do homework, play, or watch TV.

"Boy, oh boy, this terrific pen costs only 99 pfennig!" proclaims a McDonald's billboard. The fast-food chain is very popular in Germany.

Because Germany is so densely populated, many families live in apartments instead of in single-family homes. Housing can be hard to find. For that reason people tend to stay in the same homes rather than move often. Yard space is small, so many children play in the streets instead of on lawns. Even though space is tight, families still keep pets such as dogs, cats, and hamsters.

Lederhosen and *Dirndlkleide*

When you walk down the main street of Frankfurt, or any other German city, you see people dressed very much like yourself. To find traditional clothing, such as Germans wore in the past, you can attend a festival or go to a small village. In parts of Bavaria you often see older people dressed in native clothing. Men and boys wear leather shorts called lederhosen. The shorts are held up with colorful suspenders worn over a plain white shirt. They wear small green felt hats with feathers in the

A Bavarian man in traditional costume toots on his tuba during an Oktoberfest *parade.*

bands. Women wear *Dirndlkleide,* jumper-style dresses that have colorful embroidered tops covering white, lacy blouses, and full skirts. They sometimes wear bright bows or lace caps on their heads.

Dragons, Brass Bands, and Fireworks

You'll see many *Dirndlkleide* and lederhosen at the *Drachenstich,* Bavaria's oldest folk festival. Each year in August many people gather for this festival in the tiny town of Fürth im Wald. *Drachenstich* is based on a play about the slaying of a dragon. A huge dragon is pulled through the streets, belching fire through its nose (with the help of gas jets) and spewing clouds of smoke. As in most German festivals, there

A knight in shining armor reenacts a medieval tournament at Kaltenberg Castle in Bavaria.

are dancers, brass bands, parades, and much beer drinking.

Oktoberfest is another famous Bavarian festival. It was first held in 1810, in a field outside Munich, to celebrate the marriage of Crown Prince Ludwig to Princess Therese. Every year since, the citizens of Munich have repeated this celebration. Despite its name *Oktoberfest* begins in September and lasts sixteen days, ending in early October. During that time, six million people eat three-quarters of a million chickens and more than half a million sausages, and drink nearly ten million pints of beer. Brass bands play, people sing and dance, and everyone has a good time.

German farmers have always been thankful for a good harvest. They show their thanks by holding different festivals

Hundreds of people enjoy the food and drink of Oktoberfest *in a Munich beer hall.*

and events to celebrate the harvest in the fall. To the west, in the German Rhineland, heart of the country's wine-producing region, autumn is the season for wine festivals. Wine makers hold tasting sessions. Fireworks, dances, and concerts are also part of the entertainment.

Germany holds many festivals to celebrate the arts and music. In Frankfurt each autumn, the largest book fair in the world takes place. Authors, publishers, and booksellers from around the world gather to make deals and display their newest books.

The tiny town of Bayreuth (BAI-royt) in northern Bavaria is the scene each July of a grand music festival celebrating composer Richard Wagner. A similar festival is held in Bonn to honor that city's great composer Ludwig van Beethoven. The Austrian-born composer Wolfgang Amadeus Mozart (VOOHLF-gahng ah-muh-DAY-uhs MOHT-zahrt) is remembered at a festival in the Bavarian town of Würzburg.

Many festivals center around religious holidays. *Karneval* is celebrated during the spring in the Roman Catholic Rhineland of the south and west. It takes place just before Lent, when Catholics stop eating certain foods to remember the suffering of Christ. During *Karneval,* people dress in all kinds of fancy costumes and masks. They try to scare away the dark spirits of winter by cracking whips and making loud noises. Most towns also put on big parades with beautiful floats.

Easter is a very exciting holiday for German children. On the Saturday night before Easter, many towns build big bonfires, both for the Easter Sunday celebration and to welcome spring. On Sunday morning children awake to find chocolate bunnies and a nest of eggs hidden by the *Osterhase*—the Easter Bunny.

Girls wear wooden masks during Karneval.

Another important holiday for children, especially those living in the Rhineland region, is November 11. This day honors St. Martin, a rich man who one day tore his coat in two and gave half of it to a beggar. At school, children make colorful paper lanterns mounted on sticks to carry in St. Martin's Day parades. The procession is led by a man dressed as St. Martin, riding a white horse. Later the children go from house to house, singing songs in return for treats.

Three weeks before Christmas Germans celebrate the Feast of St. Nicholas. On that day, St. Nicholas (Santa Claus) arrives to hide presents in the shoes of children who have been good. Those who have been bad can expect a visit from his scary, black-robed servant, Ruprecht. Christmas is celebrated on December 24, when families decorate and light their trees. After dark, parents ring a little silver bell, the signal for children to come into the living room and open their presents. On Christmas Day families gather with relatives to eat a roast goose or turkey.

THE OBERAMMERGAU PASSION PLAY

For more than three hundred years, beginning in 1348, Europe suffered from outbreaks of a terrible disease called the Black Death. The disease was carried by rats in Europe's dirty, crowded cities, and it killed millions of people.

The people of Oberammergau (oh-buh-RAHM-uhr-gau), in the German Alps, feared the Black Death like all other Europeans did. In 1633, as it crept nearer and nearer to their town, they pleaded and prayed to God to spare them. Miraculously their prayers were answered. The Black Death stopped just short of this tiny town. So grateful were the people of Oberammergau that the next year they put on a play to thank God for sparing them.

Every ten years in Oberammergau the Passion Play is repeated. Performances begin in late May and run every day into late September. The sixteen-act, five-and-one-half-hour play tells about the last days of Jesus Christ. The stage is partially outdoors, and in the background are the beautiful Bavarian Alps. Nearly fifteen hundred people work on or perform in the play, and more than a half million visitors come to Oberammergau each year to watch it.

Lebkuchen and Other Favorite Foods

Holidays are times for German cooks to serve wonderful breads and strudel (pastries). Two favorites at Christmas are lebkuchen, a spicy Bavarian gingerbread, and stollen, a cake made with dried fruit and nuts. Sweet yeast breads are popular on St. Martin's Day. Another treat, famous in the Black Forest region, is a chocolate cake made with cherry schnapps (liquor) and covered with plump, juicy cherries and cream.

Sauerkraut (pickled cabbage) may not be your favorite vegetable. But if you like lots of starchy foods—noodles, bread, potatoes—you'll feel at home in Germany. Germans have more than two hundred different kinds of breads. You may have eaten some such as pumpernickel or German rye.

This sausage shop in Munich sells brat-wurst, weisswurst, and other unique German sausages.

The foods people eat depend somewhat on where they live. Southwestern Germans prefer spätzle (curly noodles). Bavarians like dumplings. Near the seacoast in the north fish is very popular, particularly herring and eel. The state of Nordrhein-Westphalia is famous for its smoked hams. Rhinelanders like pickled beef.

Throughout the country you'll find various kinds of sausages (wurst) such as liverwurst and the popular white sausage, weisswurst. Bratwurst (fried pork sausage) is a favorite in the state of Thüringen. The great American hot dog is also a sausage, known in Germany as the frankfurter. Around the world German wiener schnitzel (veal cutlet) is a popular meat.

For breakfast Germans often eat brötchen (bread rolls), jam, sliced meats, and cheeses. *Mittagessen,* the big meal of the day, might be meat, potatoes or noodles, bread, vegetables, and a dessert. The evening meal is lighter: bread, cheese, fruit, and perhaps a salad. In recent years Germans, like people in many other countries, have become more careful about their health. They have cut down on foods and drinks that put on weight or are bad for the heart, such as starches, pastries, fatty meats—and beer.

All ready for school, this young student totes a pretty paper cone, her Schultüten, *filled with pencils and treats.*

4

SCHOOL AND RECREATION

The Three Rs . . .
and Soccer, Too

Remember your very first day at school? Weren't you a little bit scared? Didn't you worry about where you should go and what you should do? To make that first day at school less frightening, German parents give their children *Schultüten.* These are large cones made out of colorful paper, decorated with drawings and the children's names. Inside are such school supplies as paper and pencils, along with candy, nuts, and other treats.

Different Kinds of Schools

The German word for "children" is *Kinder.* Put that with *garten*, the German word for "garden," and you have a word meaning "a garden spot where young children play and go to school." Not only is *Kindergarten* a German word, the whole idea of kindergarten began in Germany. Today kindergarten is a part of the regular school program in many countries around the world.

German children don't have to go to kindergarten, but most of them do. At the age of six they begin *Grundschule* (primary school), where they study for four years. *Grundschule* starts at 8:00 A.M. Most children walk, ride a bicycle, or take a public bus to get there. On the outside, school buildings look much like those in the United States. But inside there are fewer computers and pieces of media equipment, such as projectors and tape recorders.

German children study math, reading, writing, science, and German, along with physical education and music. Religion is also a part of the school day. Most German schools teach Christianity, either the Protestant or the Roman Catholic form. German law says that all children must have religious training until they are fourteen years old. After that they can decide whether they want to continue these classes.

At the end of *Grundschule,* children and their parents must choose among three types of schools. About a third of all students go to *Hauptschule,* similar to junior high school. Here they continue to study such subjects as math, science, and reading. They also learn skills that will help them in the working world. Most students who go to *Hauptschule* plan to go to a trade school at the age of sixteen, where they can learn how to perform jobs as different as construction work and hairdressing.

Another third of Germany's students go to *Realschule* for six years. *Realschule* prepares pupils for technical school, which they can enter at the age of sixteen. At the technical school they learn such skills as computer programming or business management.

The rest of the students go to *Gymnasium,* similar to junior/senior high school. This school offers a nine-year program for those who plan to attend a university. *Gymnasium* students must study a foreign language and certain other basic subjects.

They also begin studying in the special areas that interest them most.

There are no long summer vacations for German children. Instead they have several shorter holidays. The school year begins in late August or early September and goes until late July. There is a one-week vacation in October and two weeks at Christmas. The Easter holiday or spring break lasts three weeks, and during the religious holiday of Pentecost, fifty days after Easter Sunday, there is another one-week break.

Health Spas and Board Games

Germans watch television about two hours per day—far less than most Americans. There are some special programs for

These teenagers in Nördlingen, a town in Bavaria, entertain themselves in many of the same ways as other kids around the world.

children, but many of the cartoon shows are actually made in the United States—same characters, same scenes, different language!

When they're not watching TV, German children play games that are popular around the world, such as tag, hide-and-seek, and ball games. Board games such as chess, checkers, and Monopoly are favorites, too. One special German game, *Mensch-ärgere-dich-nicht,* is similar to pachisi. It is played by rolling dice and moving four small colored plastic cones around a board.

German workers often get a month's vacation from their jobs. Nearly half of them spend it in their own country. After Germany became united in 1990 more vacationers traveled between east and west. With the Berlin Wall gone, folks on each side were eager to see how the other lived. Outside Germany the most popular vacation spots are other European countries and the United States.

Many families like to vacation at a spa, or health resort. Germany has about 250 spas. Most are located where the air is fresh, the water clear and pure, and the climate comfortable. The word *Bad* (baht), "bath," at the beginning of a German town name usually means the town is a spa. There are different kinds of spas. One kind has public baths where people can soak in water warmed by underground springs. The minerals in the water are said to be healing. At another kind of spa people drink the water, which is rich in minerals. These kinds of spas sometimes bottle their waters and sell them in stores.

Scattered across Germany are about three thousand museums that also make good vacation stops. Visitors can see everything from the world's oldest boat to mummies, meteorites, and original works of art by world-famous painters.

Germany's highest mountain peak, the Zugspitze, is a beautiful setting for this vacation resort.

The Sports-Crazed Germans

Germans love athletics, both playing and watching. In western Germany nearly four out of ten young people belong to a club or youth organization, most of which offer sports activities. Members can play soccer, handball, volleyball, basketball,

45

FAMOUS GERMAN ATHLETES

Franz Beckenbauer (soccer) born 1945. In 1974 he was captain of the World Cup championship team. In 1990 he coached the World Cup championship team.

Boris Becker (tennis) born 1967, West Germany. At seventeen he became the youngest man ever to win a Wimbledon singles title; has since won three more. Led the West German team in two Davis Cup championships.

Kornelia Ender (swimming) born 1958, East Germany. She won four gold medals in the 1976 Summer Olympics and three silver medals in the 1972 games.

Stephanie (Steffi) Graf (tennis) born 1969, West Germany. At the age of twelve she won the tennis championship in two categories: fourteen-year-olds and under, and eighteen and under. She became an Olympic champion in 1984. In 1987 she was the best female tennis player in the world.

Roland Matthes (swimming) born 1950, West Germany. Roland set sixteen world swimming records between 1967 and 1973. At both the 1968 and 1972 Summer Olympics, he won gold medals in the 100-meter and 200-meter backstroke.

Rosi Mittermeier (alpine skiing) born 1950, West Germany. She won Olympic gold medals for downhill and slalom skiing in the 1976 Winter Olympics.

Kirstin Otto (swimming) born 1966, East Germany. Kirstin won six gold medals for East Germany at the 1988 Summer Olympics.

Katarina Witt (figure skating) born 1965, East Germany. She won gold medals in the 1984 and 1988 Winter Olympics and was a world-champion figure skater in 1984, 1985, 1987, and 1988.

Katarina Witt in 1988, the year she won a gold medal for figure skating at the Winter Olympics

tennis, or Ping-Pong. Water and track-and-field sports are also available. Teams are usually set up through the clubs rather than through the schools.

In eastern Germany only half as many young people belong to clubs, but interest is growing. When Communists ruled in the east they spent much time and money training their very best athletes for world competition. The average person did not have a chance to take part in sports. Since West and East Germany united more and more former East Germans are playing.

Soccer is the most popular German sport. The *Deutscher Fussball Bund* (*Fussball* means "soccer") is the largest sports organization in the country. Tennis is another favorite sport. Golf and horseback riding are also very popular.

For those who don't care to play team sports, Germany offers many other activities. Bicycling is popular, both as a sport and as a way to travel. Germany's mountains are among the best in the world for skiing. In summer the mountains are wonderful for hiking and rock climbing. Hikers in leather shorts and climbing boots, carrying tall walking sticks, are a common sight on the hills and mountainsides of Bavaria. Germany has thousands of miles of trails and many guides to lead visitors into the mountains. Zugspitze, the highest peak, is a popular spot both for winter sports and summer climbing.

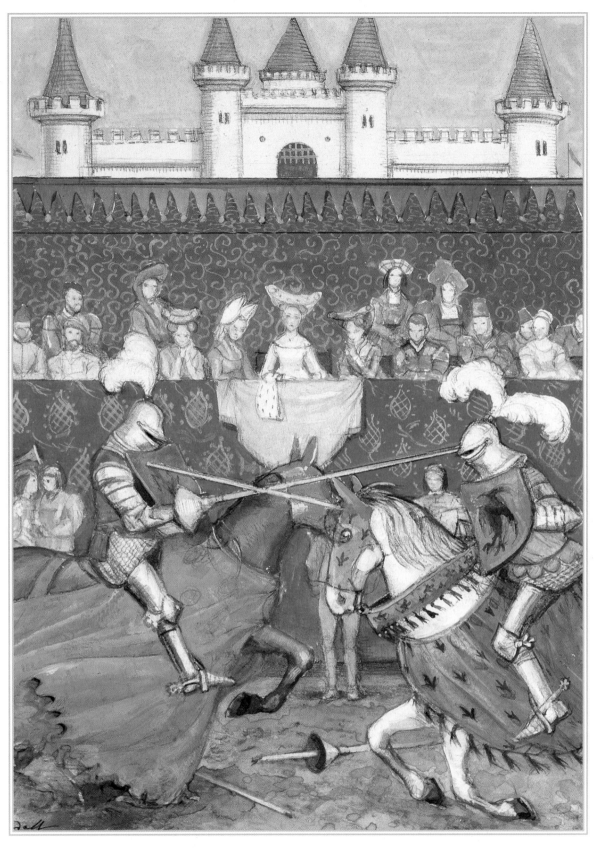

Tales of knights and their glorious deeds were popular in Germany during the Middle Ages.

5
THE ARTS

The German Spirit

Tales of Knights and Devils

The earliest stories in German were actually songs: *Volkslieder* (folk songs). Until about A.D. 750, the tales of heroes, monsters, gods, and giants were passed down by word of mouth, either in story or song. During the days of the emperor Charlemagne and the Holy Roman Empire, folktales had religious meanings. Later, in the 1100s and 1200s, German knights were powerful heroes; stories told of knights in shining armor and their lovely ladies.

In about the year 1200 a long story-poem called the *Nibelungenlied* became very popular. In the poem the hero Siegfried is killed by people who are afraid that he will become too powerful, and his large treasure is tossed into the Rhine River. Over the years the *Nibelungenlied* has been retold many times in different ways. The most famous version is a series of four operas by German composer Richard Wagner called *Der Ring des Nibelungen*. Wagner dedicated this series to his good friend and supporter, "Mad" King Ludwig II.

German writing went through great changes during the

Composer Ludwig van Beethoven

1700s. This period is called Sturm und Drang (storm and stress). Authors tried new writing ideas. Many stories praised nature and the goodness of the ordinary person. The heroes of novels and poems depended on themselves to overcome great problems in their lives.

Two writers became very famous during the Sturm und Drang period. One of them was Friedrich Schiller, Germany's finest playwright. His good friend, Johann Wolfgang von Goethe, was Germany's greatest poet. In Goethe's famous poem *Faust*, the hero makes a deal with the Devil to become young again. The Devil warns Faust that one day he will die, go to the underworld, and be doomed forever to do what the Devil says.

During the early twentieth century German authors were angry with government leaders. This was called the Revolutionary period. Its most famous writers were Heinrich Heine, Thomas Mann, and Hermann Hesse. At the same time a group of poets calling themselves "Young Germany" experimented with new ideas and modern thoughts in writing.

By the end of World War II most people did not want to talk or read about the horrors of the past seven years. A few German authors, however, did write about Hitler, the Nazis, and life in wartime Germany. Over the years, two of these authors, Günter Grass and Heinrich Böll, have taken their place among the most widely read writers in the country.

On the Stage

Germans love plays. Nearly twenty million people attend the theater each year. It's not just rich people who go. The *Volksbühne* (people's stage) lets working-class people see plays at prices they can afford.

Opera is also popular in Germany. The cities of Berlin, Munich, Stuttgart, Frankfurt, Cologne, Hamburg, and Düsseldorf all have beautiful opera houses. Opera needs an orchestra to provide its music, and there are nearly two hundred symphony orchestras in Germany. Many people say the Berlin Philharmonic is the best in the world.

Baroque, Classical, and Romantic Music

Some of the finest orchestra music was written by Germans during the Classical period—1750 to the early 1800s. One of the greatest of the Classical composers was Ludwig van Beethoven. He wrote dozens of symphonies and beautiful piano pieces.

The Classical period was not the first great age in German music. A century earlier, Johann Sebastian Bach wrote spectacular pieces for organ, piano, harpsichord, and other instruments. Bach is called the "father of Baroque," the period from 1600 to 1750. Baroque music is filled with powerful tensions and strong contrasts.

German-born composer George Frideric Handel was living in England during the Baroque period. Handel wrote many pieces for orchestra as well as religious works called oratorios. The most famous of those is *Messiah*, which church choirs often perform at Christmas.

During the Romantic age of the 1800s, Germany gave the world such great composers as Robert Schumann, Felix

Mendelssohn, and Johannes Brahms. Music in the Romantic age was not as heavy, thundering, or soul shaking as that of the Classical composers. It was more melodic and peaceful, like Brahms's "Cradle Song" ("Lullaby and good night"), which may have been sung to you when you were a baby.

OOMPAH BANDS AND YODELERS

When you think of German music you might not think of Bach, Beethoven, or Brahms. Instead, you might think of an oompah band, the kind that plays polka-style music on accordions, trumpets, trombones, and tubas. Still another kind of music that might remind you of Germany is yodeling. Yodeling is a way of singing in which the voice changes quickly from its normal tone to a high, false pitch, then back to normal again. The *yo-de-lay-ee-oh* sound is made in the throat, not with the mouth. When traveling in the Alps it is not unusual to hear the yodeling of a hiker or skier echo off the mountain peaks.

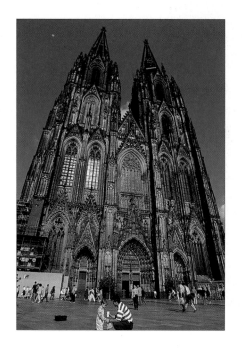

Art and Architecture

Just as the different ages of history had their own music, so did each age have its own style of art and architecture. During the 1100s, the style in Germany was Gothic. Gothic art was bold, vivid, and used many ornaments for decoration. Gothic buildings have high, steep roofs with pointed arches.

The German Renaissance, in the 1400s

The Kölner Dom (Cathedral of Cologne) is said to be the finest Gothic cathedral in Germany.

and early 1500s, was an age of "rebirth." People looked back at the past to give them ideas for the future. German architects used the structures of ancient Greece and Rome as models for new buildings. Renaissance artists added detail to their pictures so that they looked more real, almost three dimensional. Albrecht Dürer is one of the most famous artists of the time. He is known for his beautiful paintings, engravings, and

A self-portrait by German Renaissance artist Albrecht Dürer, done in 1493

This engraving of Saint Anthony was done in 1519 by Albrecht Dürer.

woodcuts—pictures made from blocks of wood carved with designs and stamped on paper.

Curving lines and heavy decoration were the architectural styles during the Baroque era from the mid-1600s to the mid-1700s. Baroque painters put patterns and a sense of rhythm into their pictures. The *Baroque Schloss* (Baroque Castle), near the town of Ettlingen, in the Black Forest, is a fine example of the architecture of the age. The castle's beautiful chapel has a spectacular domed roof. There are swirling murals painted on the plaster ceilings.

The architectural idea for which Germany is best known

St. Stephan's Cathedral in Passau is richly decorated in the Baroque style.

Little Red Riding Hood, one of the characters made famous by the Brothers Grimm

began in 1919 in the city of Weimar. The Bauhaus school of design (*Bauhaus* means "house of building") was begun by architect Walter Gropius. His goal was to combine the teaching of art, craftwork, and technology (the knowledge of tools and equipment). At the Bauhaus, painters, sculptors, designers, and architects could learn to combine their skills on one project.

The Legends Live On

If you travel to Germany today, you will see Baroque buildings, Gothic cathedrals, and art museums with Renaissance paintings. In Bonn, you can visit the *Beethovenhaus*, where the great musician was born. East of Bonn is the town of Kassel, where two hundred years ago the brothers Jakob and Wilhelm Grimm spent much of their time collecting German folktales such as "Little Red Riding Hood," "Hansel and Gretel," and "Snow White and the Seven Dwarfs." Many children in the United States and Europe grow up reading *Grimms' Fairy Tales.* Now the brothers' own story is told at the Brüder Grimm Museum.

North of Kassel is the town of Hameln, setting for the folktale "The Pied Piper of Hamelin." Back in the 1200s, many of Hameln's young men were forced to fight in a very unpopular war. As more and more of the boys disappeared from town, there were rumors that the Devil was luring them away by playing on his flute. Over the years the story changed. The Devil became a rat catcher who played his flute so beautifully that the town's rats followed him into the river and drowned. The people of Hameln were very grateful to the piper for ridding the town of rats.

Some of the rat-shaped pastries that travelers to the town of Hameln can buy as reminders of the Pied Piper

But, sad to say, they never paid him. So the angry piper lured the town's children into the river in the same way he had done with the rats—by playing on his flute.

Today if you visit Hameln, you can buy pastries in the shape of the rats. At certain times each day the town bells play the Pied Piper's song. But on the street where the story says the children followed the piper out of town, never to be seen again, no music has since been heard. . . .

Country Facts

Official Name: Bundesrepublik Deutschland (Federal Republic of Germany)

Capital: Berlin

Location: in central Europe, bordered on the north by Denmark and the North and Baltic Seas. On the east lie Poland and the Czech Republic; on the south, Austria and Switzerland; and on the west, France, Luxembourg, Belgium, and the Netherlands.

Area: 137,735 square miles (356,755 square kilometers). *Greatest distances:* east–west, 392 miles (631 kilometers); north–south, 540 miles (869 kilometers)

Elevation: *Highest:* Zugspitze, 9,721 feet (2,963 meters) in the Bavarian Alps. *Lowest:* Riepsterhammerich, 6.5 feet (2 meters) below sea level on the coast

Climate: temperate; summers mild to warm, winters cool; rainfall moderate (in all seasons)

Population: 81,088,000. *Distribution:* 34 percent live in large cities; 66 percent live in small cities and towns or rural areas.

Form of Government: federal republic

Important Products: *Agriculture:* milk, pork and beef, grains (rye, barley, wheat), grapes and other fruits, sugarbeets, and potatoes. *Industries:* automobiles, chemicals and drugs, and electronic products. *Natural Resources:* iron ore, timber, coal, potash, brown coal, and bauxite

Basic Unit of Money: deutsche mark; 1 deutsche mark = 100 pfennig

Language: German

Religion: 45 percent Protestant, 40 percent Roman Catholic, 2 percent Muslim

Flag: three horizontal stripes: black on top, red in the middle, gold on bottom. The flag displays no emblem, but an eagle appears on the country's coat of arms and on official government documents.

National Anthem: third verse of *Deutschland-Lied* ("Song of Germany")

Major Holidays: New Year's Day; Epiphany, January 6; Good Friday, Friday before Easter Sunday; Easter; Easter Monday, Monday after Easter; May Day, May 1; Ascension Day, forty days after Easter; Pentecost (or White) Monday, seven weeks after Easter Monday; Day of German Unity, June 17; Day of Prayer and Repentance, varies between November 18 and 22; and Christmas, December 25–26

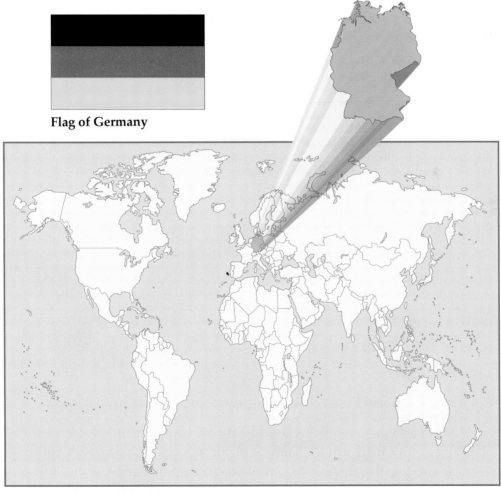

Flag of Germany

Germany in the World

Glossary

Baroque (buh-ROKE): style of art, architecture, and music that was popular in Europe from 1600 to 1750. Artists and builders used many elaborate decorations and ornaments. Music had great contrasts and powerful tensions.

Bauhaus (BOW-hous): school for architects started in Germany in 1919. It taught practical architecture that did not use fancy ornaments in building design.

communism: system of government in which all property and goods are owned by the government and are shared equally by the people. Before unification in 1990, eastern Germany was ruled by a Communist government.

democracy: system of government that is run by the people, based on their votes. In a large democracy like Germany, the people elect representatives to make laws and run the government.

Deutschland (DOYCH-lahnt): German name for Germany. The word *deutsch* or *deutsche* is the adjective that means "German."

Gothic: style of architecture that was popular in Europe from the mid-1100s through the early 1500s. Gothic buildings have high, peaked roofs with spires and pointed arches.

holocaust: total destruction by fire. When spelled with a capital "H," *Holocaust* refers to the killing of six million Jews and five million other innocent people during the time Adolf Hitler and the Nazis ruled Germany.

NAZI: these four letters are from the German words *National*

Sozialistische, which means "National Socialist." This was the political party that Adolf Hitler built into a powerful force in the 1930s and 1940s. The people who joined the party were called Nazis.

Protestant: name applied to Martin Luther and his followers who protested the teachings of the Roman Catholic Church in the 1500s. Today *Protestant* includes all types of Christian religions except Roman Catholic and Orthodox.

Prussia: very powerful state in northern Germany during the 1700s and 1800s. Prussians believed in strict discipline and lived a rigid, military way of life. Many Prussian leaders were harsh rulers who took complete power over the people.

Renaissance (REN-ih-sawns): period of history between the Middle Ages and modern times that began in Italy in the 1300s and lasted into the 1600s. In Germany, the Renaissance began in the late 1400s. It was a time of rebirth in the arts and literature, and the beginnings of modern science. Artists were inspired by the ideas of the ancient Greeks and Romans.

unification: "unifying" or "making whole." At the end of World War II, Germany was divided. For more than forty years, Communists ruled the eastern part of the country, while a free democratic republic existed in the west. On October 3, 1990, Germany became whole, or "unified," again.

xenophobia (zen-uh-FO-bee-uh): fear and dislike of foreigners, taken to extremes during Adolf Hitler's rule.

For Further Reading

Ayer, Eleanor H. *World Partners: Germany.* Vero Beach, Florida: The Rourke Corporation, 1990.

Constable, George, ed. *Library of Nations: Germany.* Morristown, New Jersey: Silver Burdett Co. and Time-Life Books, 1984.

Fuller, Barbara. *Germany,* Cultures of the World. New York: Marshall Cavendish, 1994.

Ganeri, Anita. *Focus on Germany and the Germans.* New York: Gloucester Press, 1993.

Hargrove, Jim. *Germany,* Enchantment of the World. Chicago: Children's Press, 1991.

Mayer, Mercer (illustrator). *Favorite Tales from Grimm.* New York: Four Winds Press, 1982.

Nichols, Frank. *Romantic Germany* (video). Littleton, Colorado: Quantum Communications, 1990.

Parnell, Helga. *Cooking the German Way.* Minneapolis: Lerner Publications Co., 1988.

Richter, Ken. *Portrait of Germany* (video). Littleton, Colorado: Quantum Communications, 1987.

Index

About the Author

Eleanor H. Ayer is the author of several books for young readers, including *World Partners: Germany; Cities at War: Berlin;* and *The Importance of Adolf Hitler.* She has also written about teen marriage and other social issues, and has published several biographies for young adults.

Ms. Ayer has a master's degree in literacy journalism from Syracuse University's Newhouse School of Journalism. She lives with her husband and two sons in a small town north of Denver, Colorado.